A Star to Light the Way

J. R. Ellis

No part of this publication may be reproduced, stored in a retrieval system, or transmitted in any form or by any means, electronic, mechanical, photocopying, recording or otherwise, without written permission of the publisher. For information regarding permission, write to: Grove Media, LLC. 1944 N. 820 W. Pleasant Grove, UT 84062.

ISBN: 978-1-969494-05-5

Text Copyright © 2025 by J.R. Ellis - Published by Grove Media, LLC.
All rights reserved.
Printed in the U.S.A.

**Night stretched across the heavens
like a velvet blanket, sprinkled with stars.
Each one shimmered and sparkled, lighting up the world below.**

High among them twinkled a very small star.
She hid behind wisps of cloud,
afraid that her glow was too faint to be noticed.

Every evening, the great stars gathered, boasting of their brilliance.
"I can outshine a thousand worlds," boomed one.
"My rays reach the edge of the universe!" sang another.

Little Star listened quietly.
When her turn came, she whispered,
"I only light a little town... but I do it very well."

Below, she watched her town glow softly each night.
Children used her gentle light to find their way home.
Still, she wondered, "Why would anyone need a light so small?"

So, night after night, she used her soft glow,
letting the bold stars shine...
while she tried her very best to light her little town.

Then one still evening, a golden hush fell over the sky.

**From beyond the heavens came a voice—gentle and vast.
"A holy moment has arrived," said the voice.
"My Son will soon be born upon the earth."**

Gasps rippled through the sky. The stars shimmered and bowed.
"I need a star," the voice continued,
"to guide the world to Him— to light the way to Love."

**The great stars called out at once.
"Choose me, Lord! My blaze will dazzle kings!"
"No—me! My fire burns forever!"
"Surely only the brightest can honor Your Son!"**

The voice grew quiet for a moment.
Then said softly—"Little Star."

**Little Star peeked from behind a cloud.
"Me, Lord? I'm not made for shining brightly.
I'm only a flicker compared to the other stars."**

**The other stars watched in silence.
The Little Star's heart beat faster than ever before.
She wanted to do well—but what if she failed?**

"You are kind and humble," the voice replied.
"Shine not with pride, but with love.
Love is the brightest light of all."

**She took a deep breath and whispered,
"I'll try, Lord. I'll shine with all the love that I have."**

**She focused on every kindness she had ever seen—
children sharing with each other,
a mother's song to a newborn babe,
a father praying for his family.**

**Warmth filled her, growing and spreading
until her tiny light became a bright, living glow.**

The heavens gasped as her light burst forth—soft and pure, yet strong enough to paint the earth beneath her in gold.

Down below, shepherds tending to their flocks lifted their eyes.
"Look! A new star!" one exclaimed.
"It shines brighter than all the rest."

Far away, wise men watched the heavens.
The new light shimmered in the night sky—a promise of hope,
calling them to follow.

High above them all, the Little Star shimmered joyfully.
She no longer hid.
She blazed with love, guiding the world to the Son of God.

When at last she found a small stable in Bethlehem,
her light poured down like a gentle stream.

Inside, she saw a young mother cradling her newborn son.

The Little Star hesitated, afraid her light might wake Him—
but the baby opened His eyes and smiled.
For a moment, she thought she saw her own glow reflected there.

She whispered, "I'm not the brightest light anymore, am I?"
And in her heart, she heard the Lord reply,

"No, Little Star. Now He is."

Her light softened but never faded.
Each night she watched over the world, content and full of joy.

The proud stars sparkled all around her...
but now they looked to her with wonder.
Even the grandest bowed their beams.

For they all knew that light wasn't something to keep to yourself.
It's something you share.
Something that grows brighter the more you give it away.

The Little Star's glow still shines for people all across the world.
For those with a prayer in their heart,
and for all who search for hope and peace.

"Then spake Jesus again unto them, saying, I am the light of the world: he that followeth me shall not walk in darkness, but shall have the light of life."

- John 8 : 12

www.ingramcontent.com/pod-product-compliance
Lightning Source LLC
LaVergne TN
LVHW072115070426
835510LV00002B/67